LOLLOPING LOLA *By Kirsty Shea-McKee*

Illustrations by Marisa Straccia
Doodle Press Ltd
www.doodle-press.co.uk

THE ADVENTURES OF LOLLOPING LOLA

Kirsty Shea-McKee

Illustrations
Marisa Straccia

Now you would think that Lola was an ordinary dog...

...Her archenemy Ozzy,
an ordinary mog.

But what you don't know yet,

Though they may look like
your average pet...

...When the light fades
and the moon shines bright,

A doggy adventure
begins tonight!

Just as Lola
settled down for a nap,

A screeching ball of fur
came through the cat flap.

Up Lola jumped,
what a terrible sight,

It was her archenemy, Ozzy,
as black as the night.

"Help! Help!", wailed Ozzy,
 "The children are missing."

"I need your help",
he couldn't help hissing.

Help!

Help!

Help!

Help!

Ozzy needing her help?
What a surprise,

She could tell he meant it
from the look in his eyes.

"Randal the dragon has stolen
the children from their bed,

I tried to catch him
but he had already fled.

He's taken them to his dark,
dingy cavern,

He'll save them till morning,
for breakfast he'll have 'em".

"Ok", shouted Lola,
"We must think of a plan,

To rescue our humans
as fast as we can."

"We must think of a way
to lure Randal from his cave.

We have to do this,
we must be brave".

"Locusts!", shouted Ozzy,
"He loves them to eat,

We'll find a big, juicy one,
he'll think it's a treat."

Out to the garden they ran,
as fast as they could,

And amongst the tall grass,
a locust there stood.

They captured him
in an old fishing net they found,

And ran to the cave
without making a sound.

There,
snoring loudly,
in his cave
fast asleep,

Was Randal
the dragon,
a gigantic,
great heap.

Out sprang the locust,
landing on Randal's head,

The dragon's eyes opened,
he was about to get fed.

Suddenly the locust
made off with a dash,

And off followed Randal
as quick as a flash.

"Quick children,
go as fast as you can run,

Randal's after the locust
and will soon be done".

Back at the house,
wrapped warm and tight,

The children told them
what happened that night.

"Don't worry, children,
we will keep you safe
from now on.

We will make sure
Randal the dragon stays gone".

From that night on,
when the moon shone bright,

Lola and Ozzy became friends,
much to the children's delight.

Printed in Great Britain
by Amazon